LADYBIRD ✿ HISTORIES

Ancient Egyptians

History consultant: Philip Parker, historian and author
Map illustrator: Martin Sanders

A catalogue record for this book is available from the British Library

Published by Ladybird Books Ltd
80 Strand, London, WC2R 0RL
A Penguin Company

001

ISBN: 978-0-71819-622-6
Printed in China

LADYBIRD 🐞 HISTORIES

Ancient Egyptians

Written by Brian and Brenda Williams
Main illustrations by Emmanuel Cerisier
Cartoon illustrations by Clive Goodyer

Contents

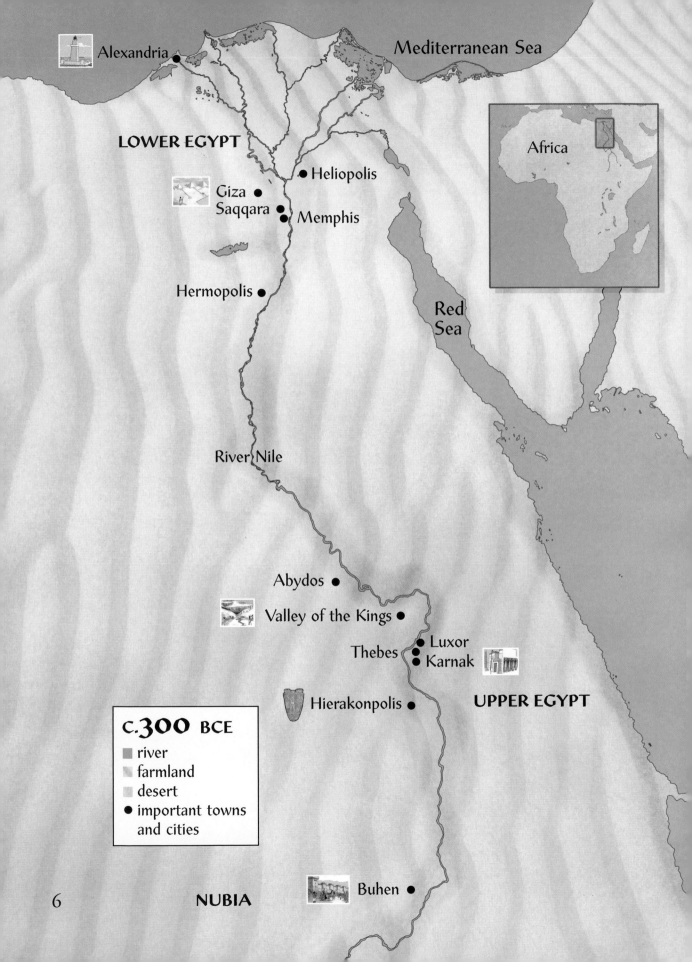

Mediterranean Sea

Alexandria

LOWER EGYPT

Heliopolis

Giza
Saqqara
Memphis

Hermopolis

Africa

Red
Sea

River Nile

Abydos

Valley of the Kings

Thebes
Luxor
Karnak

Hierakonpolis

UPPER EGYPT

C.**300** BCE
■ river
■ farmland
■ desert
● important towns
   and cities

6   **NUBIA**   Buhen ●

Timeline of Ancient Egypt

c.5500 BCE People first live and farm beside the River Nile
Predynastic period (from 4500 BCE) people live in small towns and royal palaces

c.3100 BCE **Early Dynastic Period – Dynasties 1–2**
Upper and Lower Egypt ruled by one king
First calendar and hieroglyphics

c.2686 BCE **Old Kingdom – Dynasties 3–6**
King Djoser builds the first step pyramid at Saqqara
The three Great Pyramids at Giza are built

c.2130 BCE **First Intermediate Period – Dynasties 7–10**

c.2055 BCE **Middle Kingdom – Dynasties 11–14**
By this time Egypt has a large army and rules more territory
Arts and crafts flourish, more pyramids and temples are built

c.1650 BCE **Second Intermediate Period – Dynasties 15–17**
The Hyksos from Asia and kings from Thebes rule Egypt

c.1550 BCE **New Kingdom – Dynasties 18–20**
C.1479 BCE Thutmose III is the greatest of Egypt's warrior kings
C.1340 BCE Amenhotep IV changes the religion to sun-worship
C.1336 BCE Tutankhamun becomes king (dies c.1327 BCE)
C.1279 BCE Rameses II fights the Hittites at the Battle of Kadesh
C.1100 BCE Rameses III defeats the Sea Peoples

c.1069 BCE **Third Intermediate Period – Dynasties 21–30**
Foreign kings invade and rule Egypt
C.747 BCE Egypt is ruled by King Piye of Nubia
C.600s BCE Assyrians conquer Egypt
C.300s BCE Persians rule Egypt

c.332 BCE **Ptolemaic Period**
Alexander the Great defeats Persia and rules Egypt
General Ptolemy starts a new dynasty, the Ptolemies
31 BCE Queen Cleopatra is defeated by the Romans
30 BCE Egypt becomes part of the Roman Empire

Introduction

Egypt is a big country in Africa. Its history goes back more than 5,000 years to when it was a great civilization beside the River Nile. The people of Ancient Egypt built cities, temples, palaces and pyramids. Rich families lived in fine homes with splendid gardens. Boats sailed on the Nile and out to sea, taking goods, such as papyrus and linen, from Egypt to other countries. Rulers from other lands came to offer gifts to the kings of the mighty empire of Egypt.

Egypt was called the 'Gift of the Nile' by ancient historians.

Gift of the Nile

The map on page 6 shows how the River Nile flowed through Ancient Egypt. On both sides of the river the land is hot desert but, thanks to the water of the Nile, Ancient Egypt's farmers could grow all the food its people needed. The landscape has changed little and, away from Egypt's modern cities, farmers' fields look much the same today.

Ancient Egyptians believed their gods and their kings made life possible. But without the life-giving water of the Nile this great civilization would not have lasted.

9

Builders of Pyramids

Today it is still possible to visit some of the pyramids that were built in Ancient Egypt. Inside each great pyramid a king or queen was buried. Less important people had smaller pyramids. Most ordinary people did not have pyramids at all. Instead, they were buried in the desert.

Building a pyramid was hard work. Cutting, moving and lifting the heavy stones was done by human muscle-power alone. Each pyramid took about 10,000 workers twenty years to build. Most of the work was done by peasants who worked as a way to pay tax to the king.

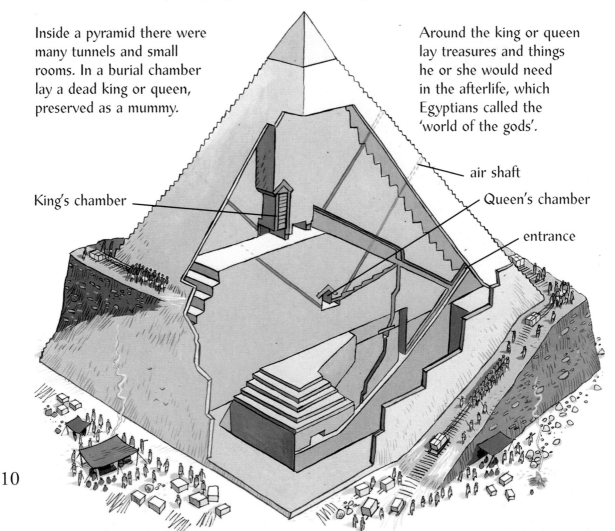

Inside a pyramid there were many tunnels and small rooms. In a burial chamber lay a dead king or queen, preserved as a mummy.

Around the king or queen lay treasures and things he or she would need in the afterlife, which Egyptians called the 'world of the gods'.

King's chamber

air shaft

Queen's chamber

entrance

Giza

The three biggest pyramids that can be found today are at Giza, near modern-day Cairo. The largest, for King Khufu, is 139 metres high. Known as the Great Pyramid, it has around 2.5 million blocks of stone. There are two slightly smaller pyramids nearby, made for Khafre (Khufu's son) and Menkaure (possibly another son). More than 130 pyramids remain in Egypt, though some are now just heaps of stones.

The average weight of a stone in the Great Pyramid was 2.5 tons. King Khufu's pyramid has lost some stones from its top and was originally 8 metres higher than it is today.

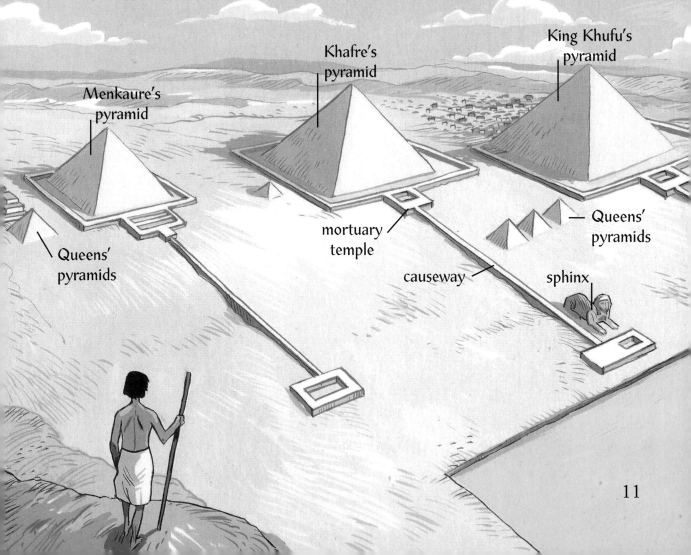

Menkaure's pyramid

Khafre's pyramid

King Khufu's pyramid

Queens' pyramids

Queens' pyramids

mortuary temple

causeway

sphinx

Land of Mystery

Ancient Egypt's civilization lasted 2,500 years, through more than thirty royal families, or dynasties. The kings of Egypt led armies to battle and built cities and temples. At first kings and queens were buried in tombs inside pyramids. Later kings decided that the pyramids took too long to build and were not safe from robbers, so they switched to rock tombs in the Valley of the Kings.

The Valley of the Kings was a large royal cemetery near Luxor.

The sphinx

Sphinxes were built to guard and protect a pyramid or temple. A sphinx has a lion's body and a human head, and is carved from solid rock. An avenue of ram-headed sphinxes guarded Amun's temple at Karnak.

The end of Ancient Egypt

After about 350 BCE Egypt did not have any more Egyptian rulers. People from other lands began to conquer and settle in Egypt. These people marvelled at its pyramids and temples, but could not understand why they had been built. The ways of Ancient Egypt, such as how to read hieroglyphics, were soon forgotten. Mummies were dug up, crushed and sold as 'magic' powder.

Ancient discoveries

Egypt was a land of mystery until the 1800s, when people found out how to read hieroglyphics and archaeologists began to uncover the remains of cities and opened tombs. The work of discovery is still going on today. Every year we find out more about the remarkable Land of the Nile.

Scribes

Scribes recorded Ancient Egypt's history. They were the only ancient Egyptians who could read and write. Scribes made lists of kings, battles and other events.

Famous sites

Archaeologists study everything from the ruins of palaces to bones, pottery, seeds and even leftover food in ancient rubbish heaps. Some of the most famous archaeologists have worked in Egypt, such as Howard Carter and Flinders Petrie.

How Ancient Egypt Began

The first people in Ancient Egypt were hunters and food-gatherers. More than 5,000 years ago people began to settle in villages along the Nile. Their rulers became Egypt's first kings.

Egypt was originally a land of two parts: Upper Egypt and Lower Egypt, and each part had its own king. Lower Egypt was in the north, where the River Nile flows into the Mediterranean Sea. Upper Egypt was in the drier region of the south. Around 3100 BCE these two parts were united by a strong soldier-king. The name of this king is uncertain. Different stories tell of kings called Menes, Narmer and Aha.

The Narmer Palette

In 1898, the Narmer Palette was discovered at Hierakonpolis. It is a picture on a tall slab of slate showing a king about to kill an enemy. The king is named as Narmer. His two crowns show he ruled both Upper and Lower Egypt.

Memphis

The strong soldier-king who united Upper and Lower Egypt built the first capital city in Ancient Egypt at Memphis – the city of merchants. Here, street traders sold their produce and boats full of goods left the city to trade with foreign countries. Many ships docked to sell precious goods from abroad, such as timber from Lebanon and silver from Syria.

Memphis was a bustling city filled with street traders, soldiers and sailors.

Dynasties

This soldier-king not only built the first capital city, he also founded Ancient Egypt's first dynasty — the first of thirty dynasties in its history. The tombs of these early dynasty kings were found at Abydos in 1900–1 by British archaeologist Flinders Petrie. Around the royal tombs he found the graves of other people, including many women who may have been the kings' servants or wives.

Old and Middle Kingdoms

Ancient Egypt had three main periods of strong kings. These were the Old Kingdom (c.2686–c.2130 BCE), the Middle Kingdom (c.2055–c.1650 BCE) and the New Kingdom (c.1550–c.1069 BCE). In between were intermediate periods when the powers of the kings grew weaker.

The Old Kingdom

During the first two dynasties, known as the Early Dynastic Period, the kings of Egypt started to build palaces and temples to the gods. Dynasties three to six ruled during the Old Kingdom. It was at this time that great kings built the first pyramids. The earliest was the step pyramid of King Djoser, built about 2620 BCE. The sides of the pyramid went up in steps rather than being smooth. The Great Pyramids at Giza, the biggest in Egypt, were built soon afterwards.

The Middle Kingdom

The Middle Kingdom began in the eleventh dynasty with King Mentuhotep I. A strong ruler, he made Thebes his capital city. Later Middle Kingdom kings conquered Nubia (modern Sudan) in the south. They sent traders and soldiers up the River Nile to build forts, in which soldiers lived and protected Egypt, and to trade with people in central Africa.

Royal badge
Kings wore a pleated skirt or loincloth and a belt with a cartouche (badge) showing their name.

Living gods

The king of Egypt was treated as a god and was seen as the son of Osiris (see page 28). He wore a false beard and on his royal headdress was a cobra that was believed to protect the king from his enemies.

As a sign of respect, ancient Egyptians would kneel before their god-king.

The New Kingdom

The New Kingdom was the greatest period in Ancient Egypt's long history. During this time Egypt was ruled by many kings, and even a queen. The New Kingdom began in about 1550 BCE, more than 3,500 years ago. It followed years of invasion and rule by foreign kings, including the Hyksos from Asia. The invaders brought new inventions with them, such as the wheel and horse-drawn chariots. Their bronze weapons were better than the stone and copper weapons of the ancient Egyptians.

The ancient Egyptians of the New Kingdom learned quickly. They soon made their own chariots and bronze swords. King Ahmose defeated the Hyksos and founded the eighteenth dynasty. For 500 years Egypt's New Kingdom was the world's strongest empire. Soldier-kings, such as Thutmose III, led large armies to conquer other lands.

Religion

In around the 1300s BCE Ancient Egypt was thrown into confusion. King Amenhotep IV decided to change Egypt's religion. He told people to worship only the sun-god Aten, rather than the many gods of the traditional religion. When King Amenhotep IV died in about 1336 BCE, Tutankhamun became king and the old gods were worshipped once more.

Kings and queens

New Kingdom kings were called pharaohs. The word 'pharaoh' comes from the Egyptian for 'great house'. New Kingdom rulers included Queen Hatshepsut and the soldier-kings Seti I and his son, Rameses II (the Great), who built many temples and palaces. Egypt spread its empire north to Palestine and Syria, and south into Nubia. Egyptian kings also fought off new invaders – the Sea Peoples. However, in about 1069 BCE the New Kingdom ended. The country was again divided and governed by foreign rulers. Ancient Egypt's greatest days were over.

Thutmose III, in his war chariot, often led his army into battle.

Greece, Rome and Egypt

Towards the end of Ancient Egypt's history a struggle for power between priests and nobles left the country weak, and foreign rulers invaded again. These invaders included Nubians from Nubia (modern Sudan), Assyrians from Mesopotamia (modern Iraq), and later Persians (from modern Iran).

In 332 BCE the Greek ruler Alexander the Great defeated the Persians and made Egypt part of his empire. He was fascinated by Ancient Egypt and even dressed as a pharaoh. He founded the city of Alexandria and built the world's biggest library and a grand lighthouse, the Pharos. After Alexander died, one of his generals, Ptolemy, founded a new dynasty in Ancient Egypt.

Alexander the Great in Alexandria, with the Pharos in the background.

Cleopatra

The last of the Ptolemy rulers was Cleopatra, Queen of Egypt. She ruled at first with her brothers, and was the first female pharaoh for more than a thousand years. In 31 BCE, she was defeated by a new Roman leader, Octavian. Cleopatra killed herself in 30 BCE, and Ancient Egypt became part of the Roman Empire.

According to legend, Cleopatra died when she let an asp, a poisonous snake, bite her.

Secrets of Egypt

For hundreds of years people have been eager to find out more about Ancient Egypt and its people. In the 1100s an Arab traveller, Abdul Latif, visited the country. In his writings he mentions seeing Egyptian men offering to climb a pyramid for a price, and traders selling mummies and statues of pharaohs, scribes and gods to make money.

Famous discoveries

In the 1600s some Europeans began to visit Egypt. They brought back stories of the pyramids and temples they had seen. Then, in the 1700s and 1800s, archaeologists began to uncover Ancient Egypt's secrets. It was after the Rosetta Stone was found in 1799, by soldiers of the French general Napoleon, that experts worked out how to read hieroglyphic writing.

The Rosetta Stone

The Rosetta Stone is a piece of ancient black stone commemorating Ptolemy V's victory against rebels in 197 BCE. On it the same inscription is written in hieroglyphics, in demotic writing and in Greek. By comparing the three writings, Thomas Young (an English scientist) and Jean-François Champollion (a French scholar) were able to break the code and unlock the secrets of the hieroglyphics.

Egyptian treasures

Treasures were taken from Egypt to museums and other places around the world. In the 1800s three obelisks were shipped to Paris, New York and London. Known as Cleopatra's Needles, they quickly became tourist attractions.

Archaeologists explored the royal burial ground, the Valley of the Kings, near Luxor. When Tutankhamun's tomb was discovered in 1922, it made headlines all over the world.

Cleopatra's Needle has stood on the bank of the River Thames in London since 1878.

Egyptian Writing

Most Egyptian people never learned to read or write. Scribes recorded Ancient Egypt's history using pictures to represent ideas and sounds. A student scribe had to learn more than 700 picture-signs. Scribes did not have to pay tax or do any farm work. They recorded details of kings and queens and stories of battles. They were responsible for counting sacks of wheat in grain stores and measuring how high the Nile flood rose each year with stone markers called Nilometers.

Reading hieroglyphics has helped us understand how people in Ancient Egypt lived. Hieroglyphs were called 'words of the gods'; they were often used for texts on monuments, especially religious ones. Priests sometimes used a quicker joined-up style of writing called hieratic. Letters and business notes were written in demotic writing.

Writing tools

Scribes would carve into stone or paint on walls in tombs. For everyday lists or letters, the Egyptians wrote on paper made from papyrus reed. They used brushes made from twigs and reed, and ink made from coloured minerals and oils.

Papyrus

Papyrus paper was made from a tall plant called papyrus. The ancient Egyptians would use the inner stem of the plant to make the paper.

Egyptian hieroglyphs

Just as our language changes and adapts today, with new words added all the time, ancient Egyptians made up new picture-signs. Here are some hieroglyphs below:

Farming

The people of Ancient Egypt called their land Kemet, meaning the 'Black Land'. This was because every year the River Nile flooded, spreading a rich, black mud over farmers' fields. When the flood went down, everyone set to work ploughing fields and planting seeds. They even dug irrigation ditches to store and carry water. Most people worked the land; only old people, scribes and priests were excused.

Farmers were called 'servants of the king'. They grew enough food for everyone: wheat and barley; vegetables, such as lettuce, cucumbers and onions; and fruits, including dates and grapes. They kept cattle, goats, ducks and geese. Many people ate fish from the river, too.

The 'Good One'

The Egyptians believed the god Osiris first showed farmers how to plant crops, and how to make bread, beer and wine. They called him the 'Good One'. Egyptians pictured the god Osiris as a farmer, with a flail and a shepherd's crook. They prayed to Osiris to make sure the Nile flood returned year after year.

Gentle flood

The Nile flood began on about the same day every year, around 19 June. The river flowed gently over the farmland, turning villages into islands. Villages were built on mounds, so houses stayed dry above the rising river.

To lift water from the river, farmers used a shaduf. It was a long pole, balanced like a seesaw, with a weight at one end and a bucket at the other.

Gods and Temples

People in Ancient Egypt believed in many gods. Gods were worshipped in temples. Here are some of the gods of Ancient Egypt:

Amun-Re
The king of the gods, originally worshipped at Heliopolis as the sun-god Re.

Ptah
The god of craftsmen and artefacts at Memphis.

Thoth
The bird-headed god of wisdom and writing, worshipped at Hermopolis.

Osiris
The god of the underworld.

Isis
The goddess of magic and life.

Horus
The god of the sky. Son of Osiris and Isis.

Amun
The god of air and wind, worshipped at Karnak.

Anubis
The god of death. He had the head of a jackal (a kind of wild dog).

Renenutet
The cobra-goddess brought a good harvest.

Sobek
The crocodile-god protected people from hungry Nile crocodiles.

Bastet
The cat-goddess of music and dancing.

Hathor
The cow-goddess watched over women.

Statues

A god's temple contained a statue of the god. The temple entrance was called the pylon. The sun's rays shone in through the pylon into the dark inside.

Only the king and priests were allowed inside temples. Priests washed and dressed the statue of the god, and offered it food and drink. Ordinary people only saw the statues of gods at festivals, when they were carried in a procession. The greatest procession was at the Festival of Opet, when the statue of the god Amun was carried in a boat down the Nile from Karnak to Luxor.

The biggest temple was the Temple of Amun at Karnak, near Thebes. Its great hall had 134 stone columns.

29

King and People

In Ancient Egypt, the king was the link between the earth-world of the people and the sky-world of the gods. The king led his army, made laws and was the chief priest. Pictures show Egyptian kings defeating enemies in battle and receiving gifts from foreign rulers. As he grew older, the king had to prove he was still strong. At the festival of Heb Sed he ran alongside a sacred Apis bull, to show he was still fit enough to rule.

The king and his relatives were at the top of ancient Egyptian society. Below them came viziers, government ministers, high priests, scribes, town mayors, doctors, soldiers, farmers, craftsmen, peasants and lastly slaves (often prisoners captured in wars).

A royal dynasty

Some kings married their sisters or half-sisters to keep the royal line pure. Rameses II had seven great wives, several lesser wives and many concubines. He possibly had as many as 100 sons and fifty daughters.

Egyptian kings spent their time travelling, hunting, fighting enemies and performing rituals at temples. The chief minister or vizier saw the king every day to receive orders. The vizier's job was to oversee Egypt's farming, irrigation, building, taxes and trade. The king sent tax collectors to farms to gather half of what each farmer grew. This food-tax was used to feed workers, soldiers and priests.

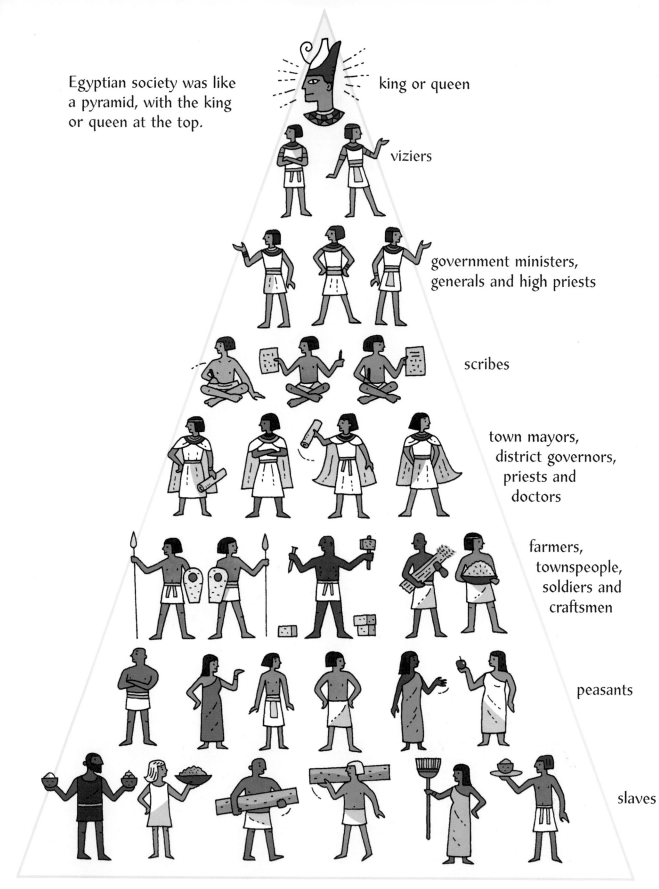

Egyptian society was like a pyramid, with the king or queen at the top.

king or queen

viziers

government ministers, generals and high priests

scribes

town mayors, district governors, priests and doctors

farmers, townspeople, soldiers and craftsmen

peasants

slaves

Mummies

Mummification was very expensive so most poor people were buried in the desert. Only the rich had painted wooden coffins and large tombs. Ancient Egyptians believed a dead person could live again in the next world, but only if the body was preserved. That is why they made mummies. They believed that the jackal-god Anubis invented mummy-making, and that he led the dead to Osiris for judgement. Each person's heart was weighed against a feather to test if they had led a good life. Those who failed Osiris's test were eaten by Ammit (a goddess who was part lion, part hippopotamus and part crocodile). They did not continue into the hoped-for afterlife.

Mummification

Making a mummy took seventy days. First, the internal organs were removed, though the heart was left so that it could be weighed by Anubis and judged by Osiris. The body was then treated with salt to dry it out and stuffed with linen, before being sewn up and treated with ointments and spices. Finally it was wrapped in bandages. After seventy days, the finished mummy was put in a wooden coffin.

Canopic jars were used to store the internal organs.

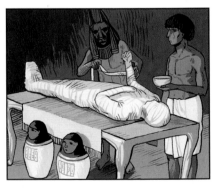
The priest in charge of making a mummy wore a jackal mask.

Sealing the tomb

A king or queen's coffin top might then have been decorated with magic spells and images of gods. The coffin was then placed inside another and another, and finally placed in a stone box, called a sarcophagus. A dead king or queen was given a splendid funeral. Crowds wept as the mummified body was taken to the royal tomb. Inside the royal tomb was everything the king or queen would need in the next world: treasure, furniture, clothes, weapons, food and drink, little models of servants (called shabti) and even bunches of flowers. Before leaving the tomb, the priests left magic signs to keep out evil spirits. Then, the entrance was sealed.

The funeral procession of a beloved king.

Mummy pets

Ancient Egyptians were fond of their pet cats and made thousands of cat mummies. They also made mummies of other animals, such as birds, crocodiles, baboons and even mice!

Pyramid Secrets

Before work began on a pyramid, an Egyptian king or queen said prayers at the site on the west bank of the Nile. Most pyramid building was done during the Nile flood, when farmers had free time.

The pyramid entrance was always built facing north. This was so that the dead king or queen would easily find his or her way to the stars. To find north the Egyptians looked for a star we call the Pole Star. They noted its position in the morning and again in the evening.

Royal burial chamber

From the outside a pyramid looked like a great white arrow pointing to the stars. Inside, it was dark and stuffy. The main tunnel led to the royal burial chamber. This is where the dead king or queen lay with their treasures after the funeral.

Despite priests and workers sealing the chamber with heavy stones and hiding the entrance, robbers often broke in. They risked being trapped inside while they tried to get at the riches. Almost every ancient Egyptian tomb was robbed over time.

Gateway to heaven

Ancient Egyptians thought that an area of night sky where the stars appeared to move was the gateway to heaven. Pyramid builders would build a shaft from the main burial chamber of a pyramid, so that the king's soul could easily find its way to heaven.

Tomb raiders risked being trapped alive inside a pyramid.

Workers and Builders

Ancient Egypt's civilization was built by an army of workers. Skilled craftsmen and tradespeople lived and worked in Egypt's cities. There were shopkeepers, metalworkers, brickmakers, weavers, butchers, bakers, shoemakers and shipbuilders.

Back-breaking work

The toughest jobs involved working deep in mines and quarries, digging up granite used for building temples. Workers were paid in food and drink. Egyptians did not use money but had special copper weights, called deben, that they used in exchange for goods. Pulling a big, heavy statue was back-breaking work that was usually carried out by slaves. A single statue might weigh 1,000 tons and need 3,000 slaves to pull it. Ox bones have been found at some tomb sites, so it is possible that oxen may also have been used to pull heavy loads.

Tomb building

In the Valley of the Kings, tomb builders lived in site villages. The workers' village at Deir el-Medina, discovered in 1905 by the Italian archaeologist Ernesto Schiaparelli, had one main street with mud-brick houses on each side.

Most workers worked for ten days, then had two days' rest. They took a lunch break at noon. Tools were handed out and weighed at the start of the day, and weighed again at the end. A scribe made sure no valuable copper was stolen. He locked up the tools every night. Any worker who did steal was beaten with a stick.

Scribes counted valuable tools at the start and end of each working day.

37

Home Life

Most poor Egyptian homes were small and overcrowded. They made do with a house of just three or four rooms. Rich people had big houses with lots of rooms, a courtyard and gardens. They had wooden beds, chairs and tables, stands for oil lamps and vases of flowers.

The king had a magnificent palace for public ceremonies, and a luxurious private palace for his family. Palace rooms had walls painted with animals, trees and flowers, and there were huge gardens with lakes to relax in.

A rich Egyptian's house was large and elegant.

Inside a home

Most Egyptian homes had low walls along the edge of a flat roof, called a parapet, which pushed air downwards, creating a cool storage space inside. Door openings faced north to catch the cooling breeze, which they called the 'breath of Amun'. Some homes had only one window, so while inside was dark, the rooms were cool. The family often kept their stores of food in a small walled yard. Furniture was simple: just stools and mud-brick platforms or mats to sleep on.

Many families washed in the Nile, but a lucky few had bathrooms with piped water and a servant to give them a shower by tipping a jug of water over them. People carried drinking water in jars from wells or from the river. The toilet was a box of sand or a clay pot with a wood or stone seat.

Many poor families used the inside of their home as a shop. Some people kept a goat or geese in the front room.

Food and Drink

People in Ancient Egypt ate well. In years of good harvests few people went hungry. Bread was the main food, often eaten with vegetables. People baked fresh bread every day, sometimes adding nuts, spices, honey or dates. Only rich families drank wine. For those who could afford them, favourite meat dishes were beef, mutton (sheep) and goat.

Ancient Egyptians made cooking fires from burned charcoal, dry reeds or dried animal dung. The kitchen at the back of the house did not have a roof, so the smoke drifted away. Some families even cooked on the roof of the house as it was a safe place for a fire.

Ancient Egyptians used pet cats to hunt wild ducks in the marshes beside the Nile.

Sweet treats

Egyptians did not have sugar but kept bees for honey to sweeten dishes. They loved date and honey cakes shaped like little pyramids. Cooking oil came from the moringa or drumstick tree, and from flax plants. Later, when olive trees were introduced, the Egyptians used olive oil like the Greeks and Romans.

Hunting

Hunting animals out in the desert, such as leopard and gazelle, was a rich person's sport. But both rich and poor hunted birds such as ducks, geese, quail and pigeons for food. To kill or catch the birds, hunters threw weighted sticks at them or used nets to trap them. They also caught fish in the Nile, but kept clear of dangerous hippos!

Egyptian Women

Women had quite a lot of independence in Ancient Egypt: a woman could divorce her husband and run her own business. We know there were female bakers and weavers, for example. From about 1000 BCE to 600 BCE a woman was head-priestess at the Temple of Amun.

Egyptian goddesses

 Isis taught women the skills needed to run a home and raise a family. She showed women how to grind grain into flour, how to spin and weave cloth, and how to nurse the sick.

 Another goddess special to women was Hathor, goddess of motherhood, love, beauty and music.

Professional women

An Egyptian woman could not be forced to marry a man she did not like, and she could own her own property. She could also have a job. Nebet, a governor's wife, was a magistrate, while Peseshet, another professional woman, is named as 'overseer of physicians' on her tomb. From this it is clear she knew a lot about medicine.

Home life

Only a few women were educated. Most girls stayed at home and learned to cook, sew, clean, weave cloth and grow food. When they were old enough, usually about thirteen years of age, they married. Parents probably arranged marriages with suitable men. By the age of thirty many women were grandmothers!

Women from poor families looked after the home, washing and mending worn-out items of clothing. Rich women did not need to do such heavy work. They sent their washing to the laundry – we can even read some of their laundry lists today!

Egyptian women would wash their clothes in the River Nile.

Egyptian Children

Ancient Egyptians often had large families. Most young children ran about naked in the hot sun. Boys had shaved heads, except for a long plait at the side. This was cut off when a boy reached manhood at thirteen years old.

Children from poor families helped around the house, in the fields and in workshops. Boys often learned the same trade as their father. Only rich children, mostly boys, had lessons at home or at temple schools. They learned reading, writing, history and maths, and about Egyptian gods and foreign lands.

Toys

Children's toys included balls made from animal-skin, string puppets, dolls and toy animals on wheels. Favourites were toy lions and crocodiles with snapping jaws!

Children played outside in the hot Egyptian sun.

Slowed down

Naughty boys were often beaten by their teachers. One boy who ran away from lessons had blocks of wood tied to his ankles. He couldn't run away so quickly the next time!

Lucky charms

Ancient Egyptians wore lucky charms, or amulets, to protect themselves from accidents. A child might wear a pendant shaped like a fish to protect her in case she fell in the river.

Childhood pets

Tomb paintings show ancient Egyptian people kept dogs and cats as pets. Royal children had more exotic pets, such as cheetahs, baboons and tropical birds. Tutankhamun had a whole zoo in his palace as he grew up!

Clothes and Leisure

Just like Egypt today, Ancient Egypt was hot for most of the year, so people had to dress to stay cool. Clothes were made of linen from the flax plant. Flax stalks were soaked in water to soften them, then the fibres were combed out in thin strands. The strands were spun (twisted) to make thread, which was woven into cloth on a loom.

Men wore skirts like kilts or loincloths. Women wore long, flowing dresses. Rich women wore dresses so fine they were see-through. Most people went barefoot or wore sandals.

In the dry, sandy land, rich people kept their skin moist with oils and perfumes. Both men and women wore eye make-up – black on the upper lid, green on the lower lid – and jewellery, such as necklaces and earrings.

Wealthy Egyptian men and women liked to wear elegant jewellery and bold eye make-up.

Games and fun

Families played board games, such as senet. They liked music, stories and dancing, too. Dancers and acrobats entertained at parties. Archery and wrestling were popular sports. Out in the desert, rich men and soldiers hunted ostriches, antelope and lions. Living beside a river meant many people were good swimmers and excellent fishermen. Some even risked their lives hunting crocodiles!

Lion hunting was considered an exciting sport to watch.

Looking beautiful

Wigs were very popular in Ancient Egypt for those who could afford them. At parties, women would put a cone of fat or wax, mixed with perfumed oils, on top of their wig. As the cone melted, cooling perfume trickled down over the face and neck.

Science and Art

Ancient Egyptians were good at maths and art, and Egypt's doctors were famous for their skill and knowledge. They learned about the human body from mummy-makers. Doctors set broken bones, treated wounds and made medicines.

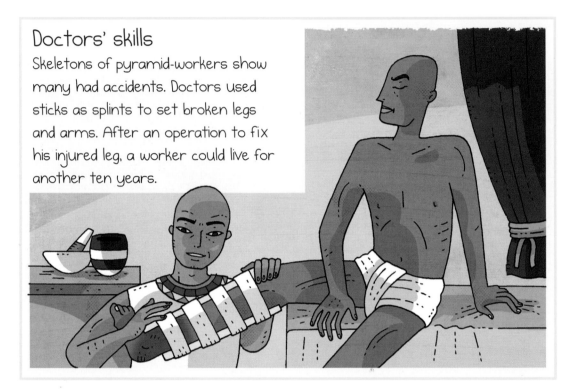

Doctors' skills

Skeletons of pyramid-workers show many had accidents. Doctors used sticks as splints to set broken legs and arms. After an operation to fix his injured leg, a worker could live for another ten years.

Astronomers studied the stars. They divided day and night into hours, each hour named after a god. To measure time they used sun-dials and water-clocks – pots with hour marks from which water dripped through small holes.

Many ancient Egyptians were good at practical sums, such as measuring areas, distances and weights. They used maths in building, trade and settling disagreements, such as who owned which plot of farmland.

The arts

Paintings on the walls of tombs give a colourful view of ancient Egyptian life, but each painting also had magical meaning. People believed the drawings would help the dead person's spirit (soul) find its way through the underworld to be reunited with the body.

Carvings in temples showed kings winning battles. There were huge stone statues of kings and gods, and small painted figures of soldiers, farmers and servants drawn on walls in tombs.

The ancient Egyptians decorated the walls of tombs with beautiful paintings.

Egyptian Battles

Egyptian kings led their armies into battle. We know what ancient Egyptian soldiers looked like from wall-pictures found in temples and from model soldiers uncovered in tombs. The first Egyptian soldiers had weapons (spears, daggers and swords) made of stone or copper. By the end of the Old Kingdom, soldiers had better weapons of bronze, and iron weapons were in use during the New Kingdom. Some soldiers carried battle-axes. But axes decorated with pictures of hunting scenes were probably used for parades, not fighting. Iron swords were best; the Egyptians called iron the 'metal from heaven'.

Ancient Egypt's forts had walls up to 40 metres high. A large fort at Buhen had 2,000 soldiers and a small town within its walls.

Soldiers at war

Soldiers sailed boats along the River Nile and travelled across the desert to conquer other lands. They built forts with mud-brick walls. Some soldiers were volunteers, but most were farmers who went to war when their king ordered them to and returned home when the fighting was over. After a victory, soldiers were given land, silver or even an enemy prisoner as a slave.

Bravery

Soldiers who fought very bravely were given a medal called the Gold Fly.

Ships and Trade

Ancient Egyptians made long journeys by land and sea. They went to trade, to conquer new lands and to bring back treasures for their kings. Some of the world's first sea-going ships were built in Egypt. Made of wood and reeds, the boats were held together with ropes and wooden pegs. Pictures show canoes with paddles and ships with sails for use on the Nile, at sea and in battles, too.

It was easier to travel by boat than over land, because there were no good roads. Donkeys carried loads on their backs and carts were pulled by oxen.

Trading ships

About 1450 BCE, Queen Hatshepsut sent trading ships to the Land of Punt – possibly the land we call Somalia today. Pictures in a temple at Deir el-Bahri, near the Valley of the Kings, show the vessels were about 30 metres long. The scribe Ineri wrote about even bigger ships on the Nile, made for carrying heavy stone obelisks. They were 70 metres long and each one was towed by thirty rowing boats.

An example of trading ships on the busy Nile river.

53

Tombs and Treasures

Interest in the secrets of Ancient Egypt grew in the 1800s as more tombs were discovered. Archaeologists studied the pyramids at Giza, the royal tombs at Saqqara, the temples at Karnak, and the Valley of the Kings near Luxor, where the later kings of Egypt were buried.

Braving the heat

In the 1800s British archaeologist Flinders Petrie took off all his clothes to work inside the Great Pyramid. It was so hot his can of tinned food melted!

The Book of the Dead

The Book of the Dead was a collection of magic spells written on papyrus scrolls, with pictures. Copies were left in tombs to help the dead pass safely into the next world.

Archaeology

Today archaeologists take great care to make sure that evidence is not lost. Sites are protected and precious objects preserved. But some of the first finds were made by treasure-hunters who did not care what damage they did. Most tombs were empty by the time archaeologists found them, having already been robbed of their treasure. But one had escaped the tomb-raiders…

Tutankhamun

The most famous tomb story began in around 1327 BCE with the death of a young king. His name was Tutankhamun. Though not one of Egypt's great rulers, he was buried in the Valley of the Kings. A gold mask was placed on his mummy and his tomb was closed. It remained sealed for more than 3,000 years, and unlike most tombs it had not been stripped bare.

In 1922 British archaeologist Howard Carter found steps leading to an unknown tomb. A few earlier clues had already been found – a cup with Tutankhamun's name and some pottery. In February 1923 Carter dug his way into the burial chamber. Inside was the richest find yet… Tutankhamun's tomb still filled with treasure!

Robbers had managed to get inside Tutankhamun's tomb, but they must have been scared away, leaving most of its contents behind.

What did the Ancient Egyptians do for us?

Ancient Egypt was one of the first great civilizations. Visitors to Egypt in the centuries that followed were impressed and wanted to know more. Why were the pyramids there? What was the mysterious picture-writing? Egypt seemed to be a land of magic and mystery, and people were fascinated.

From its tombs and pyramids we have learned a lot about Ancient Egypt. Inside Tutankhamun's tomb 5,398 objects were found, covering every aspect of ancient Egyptian life, from weapons and chariots to musical instruments, clothes, cosmetics and, of course, Tutankhamun's gold burial mask. Today tourists visit Egypt to see these pyramids and temples, and to look at the treasures at the Egyptian Antiquities Museum in Cairo. Through the work of archaeologists, historians and scientists, we can see how much other civilizations, and even the modern world, owes to Ancient Egypt.

Irrigation
Farmers used the River Nile to farm their dry land and feed lots of people.

Religion
Egypt had one of the first religions based on a belief in life after death.

Calendar

Ancient Egyptians had a 365-day calendar, just as we do today.

Building and engineering

The ancient Egyptians built cities, temples and, of course, pyramids.

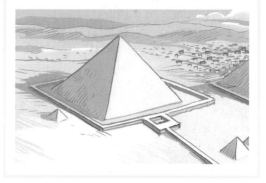

Medicine

Ancient Egypt's doctors knew a lot about how the body worked.

Writing and paper

Ancient Egyptians invented some of the earliest forms of writing, and made paper from papyrus reed.

Maths

The ancient Egyptians were very good at maths, especially geometry.

Water exploration

The Egyptians made big sailing ships, and some of the first sea-going ships were built in Egypt.

Ancient Egyptian Rulers

Listed here are some of the greatest kings and queens who ruled across thirty dynasties.

Early Dynastic Period

1st Dynasty c.3100–c.2890 BCE
Narmer / Aha / Menes c.3100

2nd Dynasty c.2890–c.2686 BCE
Hetepsekhemwy   c.2890
Peribsen   c.2700
Khasekhemwy   c.2686

Old Kingdom

3rd Dynasty c.2686–c.2613 BCE
Sanakht   c.2640–c.2637
Djoser   c.2630–c.2611

4th Dynasty c.2613–c.2494 BCE
Khufu   c.2589–c.2566
Khafre   c.2558–c.2532
Menkaure   c.2532–c.2503

5th Dynasty c.2494–c.2345 BCE
Userkaf   c.2494–c.2487
Unis   c.2375–c.2345

6th Dynasty c.2345–c.2130 BCE
Pepi I   c.2321–c.2287
Pepi II   c.2278–c.2184

First Intermediate Period

7th–10th Dynasties c.2130–c.2055 BCE
Period of weaker rule in Ancient Egypt when there were many temporary rulers.

Middle Kingdom

11th Dynasty c.2055–c.1985 BCE
Mentuhotep II   c.2055–c.2004
Mentuhotep III   c.2004–c.1992
Mentuhotep IV   c.1992–c.1985

12th Dynasty c.1985–c.1795 BCE
Amenemhat I   c.1985–c.1955
Sesostris I   c.1955–c.1920
Amenemhat IV   c.1814–c.1805
Sobekneferu (Queen)   c.1799–c.1795

13th and 14th Dynasties c.1795–c.1650 BCE
Minor kings and queens rule Ancient Egypt.

Second Intermediate Period

15th–17th Dynasties c.1650–c.1550 BCE

Ancient Egypt was ruled by more than thirty kings, including Hyksos kings from Asia.

New Kingdom

18th Dynasty c.1550–c.1295 BCE

Ahmose I	c.1550–c.1525
Amenhotep I	c.1525–c.1504
Thutmose I	c.1504–c.1492
Thutmose II	c.1492–c.1479
Thutmose III	c.1479–c.1425
Hatshepsut (Queen)	c.1473–c.1458
Amenhotep II	c.1427–c.1400
Amenhotep III	c.1390–c.1352
Amenhotep IV	c.1353–c.1336
Tutankhamun	c.1336–c.1327

19th Dynasty c.1295–c.1186 BCE

Rameses I	c.1295–c.1294
Seti I	c.1294–c.1279
Rameses II (the Great)	c.1279–c.1213

20th Dynasty c.1186–c.1069 BCE

Rameses III–XI	c.1184–c.1069

Third Intermediate Period

21st–30th Dynasties c.1069–c.343 BCE

Rulers from outside Egypt included the Libyan Sheshonk, the Kushite from Nubia and the Assyrian Necho.

Persian Period c.343–c.332 BCE

Period of rule by Persian rulers.

Ptolemaic Period c.332–30 BCE

Alexander the Great	c.332–c.323
Ptolemy I	c.305–c.285
Ptolemy V	c.205–c.180
Cleopatra (Queen)	51–31

Ancient Egypt became part of the Roman Empire in 30 BCE.

You will come across different dates in other books and sources about Ancient Egypt. Dates are based on old king lists, which are often incomplete, as well as modern research.

Glossary

Ancient Egypt	the period of Egypt's history between 3100 BCE and 30 BCE
archaeologist	a person who finds out about the past from old objects
BCE	these letters are used in dates, for example 100 BCE stands for '100 years before the common era'. CE is used in later dates, for example 100 CE stands for '100 years after the common era'
bronze	a metal made by mixing copper and tin
burial ground	a place where the dead are buried
canopic jar	a special container used to store the internal organs from a dead body during the mummification process
capital city	a country's centre of government
cartouche	an oval-shaped badge with a king's name written on it
cemetery	an area of land where the dead are buried
chariot	a two-wheeled cart pulled by horses
civilization	a way of life with rules and customs that lasts a long time
coffin	a box that a dead body is put in
concubine	an unofficial wife
copper	a soft metal
demotic writing	a form of quick writing used for everyday messages

divorce	ending a marriage by law
dynasty	a royal family, in a line of succession
empire	lands ruled by one strong country
flail	a tool used in farming
funeral	a ceremony to mark the end of someone's life
god	a supernatural being believed to affect or control life on earth
hieratic writing	a simplified form of hieroglyphics
hieroglyphics	picture-writing used to build up words in ancient Egyptian script (a hieroglyph is one picture)
inscription	writing cut into stone
invasion	an attack on one country by another
irrigation	using water from rivers to help crops grow better
loom	a machine for weaving cloth
mortuary	a place where dead bodies are kept before burial
mummy	a dead body that has been treated to preserve it
noble	someone of high rank, such as a king's cousin or uncle
obelisk	a tall stone column with a square base and sloping sides, rising to a pointed tip

Glossary

papyrus	a tall reed that grows on the edge of the Nile – used to make baskets, sandals and paper-like scrolls
pharaoh	the title given to rulers of Ancient Egypt's New Kingdom
priest	a person who carries out religious duties
pylon	two towers and the doorway between them that marks the entrance to a temple
pyramid	a stone structure built as a royal tomb
sarcophagus	an elaborate outer stone coffin
scribe	an important person in Ancient Egypt whose job was to read and write
senet	a board game with thirty squares – the original rules are unknown
shaduf	a pole with a bucket and counterweight, used to raise water from the River Nile
sphinx	half-animal, half-human mythical creature
step pyramid	a pyramid with stepped, rather than smooth, sides
sun-dial	a shadow-clock that shows the time as the sun casts a shadow on a disc marked with the hours
temple	a place of religious worship where a god's statue is kept
tomb	a special room or rock-cave in which a body is buried
trader	someone who buys and sells things

underworld	the world of the dead, thought to lie under the Earth
vizier	an official who reported directly to Ancient Egypt's king or queen

Places to Visit

The British Museum, London
The Ashmolean Museum, Oxford
The Fitzwilliam Museum, Cambridge
National Museum of Scotland, Edinburgh
Sir John Soane's Museum, London
Bristol Museum and Art Gallery, Bristol
The Manchester Museum, Manchester
The Burrell Collection, Glasgow

For more information about Ancient Egypt
and other resources, visit **www.ladybird.com**

Index